STECK-VAUGHN
PORTRAIT OF AMERICA

Nebraska

Steck-Vaughn Company

Executive Editor	Diane Sharpe
Senior Editor	Martin S. Saiewitz
Design Manager	Pamela Heaney
Photo Editor	Margie Foster
Electronic Cover Graphics	Alan Klemp

Proof Positive/Farrowlyne Associates, Inc.
Program Editorial, Revision Development, Design, and Production

Consultant: James E. Potter, Historian, Nebraska State Historical Society, Lincoln

Published by Raintree Steck-Vaughn Publishers, an imprint of Steck-Vaughn Company.

A Turner Educational Services, Inc. book. Based on the Portrait of America television series by R. E. (Ted) Turner.

Cover Photo: Chimney Rock by © Superstock.

Library of Congress Cataloging-in-Publication Data

Thompson, Kathleen.
    Nebraska / Kathleen Thompson.
        p. cm. — (Portrait of America)
    "Based on the Portrait of America television series"—T.p. verso.
    "A Turner book."
    Includes index.
    ISBN 0-8114-7347-3 (library binding).—ISBN 0-8114-7453-4 (softcover)
    1. Nebraska—Juvenile literature. I. Title. II. Series: Thompson,
Kathleen. Portrait of America.
F666.3.T46 1996
978.2—dc20   95-30031
                                        CIP
                                        AC

Printed and Bound in the United States of America

1 2 3 4 5 6 7 8 9 10 WZ 98 97 96 95

Acknowledgments
The publishers wish to thank the following for permission to reproduce photographs:
P. 7 © Donovan Reese/Tony Stone Images; p. 8 © James Blank/Tony Stone Images; p. 10 Joslyn Art Museum; pp. 11, 13 Nebraska Department of Economic Development; p. 14 Nebraska State Historical Society, Solomon D. Butcher Collection; p. 15 North Wind Picture Archive; p. 16 (top) © John Carbutt/Union Pacific Museum Collection, (bottom) Nebraska State Historical Society, Solomon D. Butcher Collection; p. 17 Nebraska State Historical Society; p. 18 Colorado Historical Society; p. 19 Nebraska State Historical Society; p. 20 © Michael Reagan; p. 21 Courtesy the Belville family; p. 22 © Donovan Reese/Tony Stone Images; p. 24 (top) © Michael Reagan, (bottom) Valmont; p. 25 (top) Nebraska Wheat Board, (bottom) Hormel Foods Corporation; p. 26 Nebraska Department of Economic Development; p. 27 Homestead National Monument, National Park Service; p. 28 Nebraska Department of Economic Development; p. 29 Courtesy Shirley Johnson; p. 30 Nebraska State Historical Society, Willa Cather Pioneer Memorial Collection; pp. 32, 33 Nebraska State Historical Society; p. 34 Nebraska Game & Parks Commission; p. 35 (top) The Bettmann Archive, (bottom) UPI/Bettmann; pp. 36, 37, 38, 39 (both) © Boys Town; pp. 40, 41 Pioneer Village; p. 42 © Mark Gibson/Southern Stock; p. 44 Nebraska Department of Economic Development; p. 46 One Mile Up; p. 47 (left) One Mile Up, (center) North Dakota Tourism, (right) © Earth Scenes.

STECK-VAUGHN
PORTRAIT OF AMERICA

Nebraska

Kathleen Thompson

WINNEBAGO TRIBAL LIBRARY
WINNEBAGO, NEBRASKA

A Turner Book

RSVP
RAINTREE
STECK-VAUGHN
PUBLISHERS
The Steck-Vaughn Company

Austin, Texas

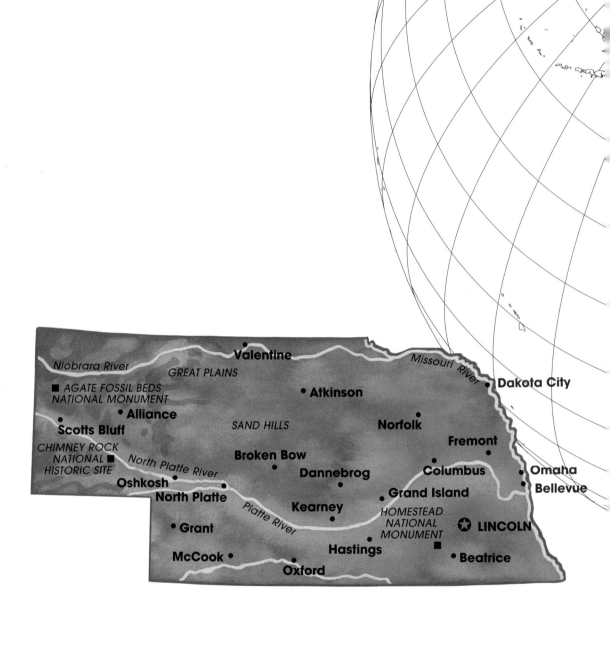

Nebraska

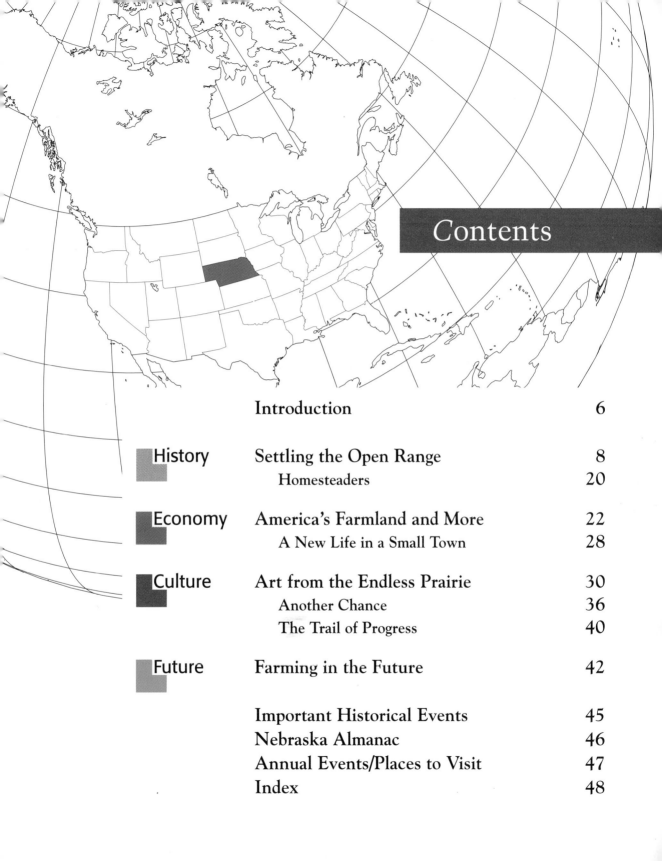

Contents

Introduction

True pioneer spirit means hard work, strength, and determination. Nebraska stands as an example of such pioneer spirit. Many early settlers crossed Nebraska's Great Plains heading west to California and Oregon. Only the hardiest pioneers dared to stay on in Nebraska. Explorers who passed through this land on their way to the West called it the "Great American Desert." Much of Nebraska is naturally dry and sandy. Although farmers had a hard time raising crops, these were not the type of people who gave up easily. They irrigated the land and planted trees across the state. The green, rich Nebraska of today shows what true pioneer spirit can do.

These fountains contrast the image of the state once better known as part of the "Great American Desert." The Heartland of America Park fountains are in Omaha, next to the Missouri River.

Nebraska

Boys Town, Platte River, homesteaders

Settling the Open Range

Archaeologists have gathered evidence showing that Native Americans lived in present-day Nebraska at least 11,000 years ago. Very little is known about these people—only that they hunted wildlife and gathered edible plants. By the 1500s the Native Americans had divided up into smaller groups. Some of them, such as the Sioux, Arapaho, Cheyenne, and Comanche, lived by hunting the herds of buffalo that lived on the vast, dry grassland known as the Great Plains. Native Americans hunted buffalo not only for their meat but also for their skins. In fact the entire animal was used. The Native Americans hung the meat to dry in the sun as a way of preserving it. The skins were used to make blankets and robes. Buffalo bones were carved into knives; hooves and horns were boiled into glue. Native Americans even used the buffalo's tendons for bowstrings. Because Native Americans relied on the buffalo so much, their custom was to thank the slain animal for providing for their needs.

Nebraska's state capitol building in Lincoln has a four-hundred-foot central tower. The city was originally named Lancaster, but it was renamed in honor of Abraham Lincoln.

This watercolor by Alfred Jacob Miller depicts Native Americans hunting buffalo at Independence Rock.

These Native American groups were nomads. They lived in temporary villages, moving along with the seasonal migrations of the buffalo herds. Other groups, who lived in the river valleys, were more settled farming people. These were the Missouri, Omaha, Oto, Pawnee, and Ponca. These groups lived in villages and raised crops. They also hunted the buffalo, usually leaving their villages twice a year for that purpose.

In 1541 the Spanish explorer Francisco Vásquez de Coronado and his men traveled across the southwestern part of what is now the United States. He was looking for gold, but he didn't find it. Coronado traveled as far north as present-day Kansas before he turned back. Still he claimed the entire region, including present-day Nebraska, for Spain.

In 1682 René-Robert Cavelier, Sieur de La Salle, and his men traveled down the Mississippi River to the Gulf of Mexico. He claimed all the land drained by the river for France. This claim included the region of Nebraska. Both Spain and France had claimed the area of Nebraska, although no European had ever set foot there.

In 1714 a European explorer actually did reach the area. He was the French explorer Etienne Veniard de Bourgmont. He made his way up the Missouri River to the mouth of the Platte River in eastern Nebraska. Not long after that, French fur traders followed his route. The land was rich in beaver, and furs were in great demand in Europe. The traders bargained with the Native American people for beaver pelts.

In the early 1700s, the Spanish began to object to France's presence in the area. They had claimed this land over a hundred years before the French. Although they had never actually visited it, the Spanish didn't like the French traders taking furs from territory Spain claimed. In 1720 the Spanish sent a force led by Pedro de Villasur to stop the French. He led his soldiers overland from Santa Fe, in what is now northern New Mexico. As they reached the vicinity of present-day Columbus, they encountered a group of Pawnee. The Spanish were accustomed to easy victories over the Native Americans. But the Pawnee warriors were too much for them. Villasur and many of his men were killed in the battle.

After the fur traders, the next Europeans to travel across present-day Nebraska were two French brothers. In 1739 Pierre and Paul Mallet traveled up the Missouri River, which forms the eastern

Elk browse at the Fort Niobrara National Wildlife Refuge, near Valentine in far north-central Nebraska. Scenes such as this one must have greeted early Spanish and French explorers.

border of Nebraska. They stopped at an area near present-day Sioux City, Iowa, and retraced their route back to the Platte River. They followed the river westward to the central portion of present-day Nebraska. Then they turned south and journeyed to Santa Fe. Their exploration strengthened French claims to this area.

In 1763 France transferred to Spain the rights to all the land La Salle had claimed. In 1800 Spain returned the land to France. Three years later France sold the land west of the Mississippi River to the United States. This sale, known as the Louisiana Purchase, doubled the size of the new nation. One year later, President Thomas Jefferson chose Meriwether Lewis and William Clark to explore the new territory and look for a water route to the Pacific Ocean. The expedition, which included Native American guides, journeyed northwest along the Missouri River.

Another explorer was sent by John Jacob Astor, a New York merchant who had built a fur-trading empire in the Pacific Northwest in the early 1800s. Astor had built forts and sent in armed men to protect his access to the valuable furs. At that time the most common way to transport furs to New York was to ship them by boat around the tip of South America. In 1812 Astor sent a man named Robert Stuart to find an overland route across the continent. The West was wilderness then, and much of it was desert. Stuart had to find a route with enough water that was easy enough to travel so that shipments of furs could be transported safely. The route that Stuart pioneered followed the

North Platte and Platte rivers—straight across present-day Nebraska. In the following years, this route became part of the Oregon Trail. Between 1843 and 1869, more than 350,000 people traveled the trail westward toward California, Oregon, and Washington.

Still the settlement of Nebraska proceeded very slowly. Many people passed through, but few stayed. In 1819 the United States Army built Fort Atkinson on the banks of the Missouri River, near present-day Omaha. Fort Atkinson provided Nebraska with its first school, first library, and first sawmill. However, the fort was considered too far into the wilderness to be worthwhile. It was shut down in 1827.

Other Americans came to explore the land, but most of them were unimpressed. They looked at the vast expanse of grassland and thought it was useless. But there were still furs to be found. In 1823 Bellevue was established as a fur-trading post on the Missouri River, a little way south of Fort Atkinson. Bellevue became Nebraska's first permanent town.

By the 1830s Nebraska had its first wave of new immigrants. They weren't European settlers, however. They were Native Americans. As Americans settled the land east of the Mississippi River, the Native

Pioneering enthusiasts in authentic costumes re-create a camp scene from the days of the Oregon Trail.

Trees for lumber were very scarce on the Nebraska prairie, so early settlers and homesteaders lived in sod houses such as this one.

Americans living there were pushed off their traditional lands. Americans used the land west of the Mississippi River as one big reservation. The United States government promised the Native Americans that their new territory would belong to them forever. Nebraska became the home of the Santee Sioux, the Winnebago, and the Omaha.

By 1843 settlers were following the Oregon Trail to the West. Thousands of pioneers made their way across the land promised to Native Americans. The Native Americans seldom fought with the pioneers, however. As long as the pioneers did not stay, they did not trouble the Native Americans.

The situation began to change in the 1850s as more and more wagon trains pushed through to the West. Some pioneers began settling in the Platte River valley that had been farmed by the Native Americans. In 1854 the United States Congress passed a bill making present-day Kansas and Nebraska government territories. More and more settlers moved onto Native American lands and then called on the United States Army to protect them. In 1854 there were 2,732 settlers living in Nebraska. Six years later there were 28,841. In another ten years there were 122,993.

In 1861 eleven states in the South withdrew from the Union. The major issues involved in the dispute were slavery and states' rights. The resulting Civil War did not affect the Nebraska Territory greatly, as it was far out on the frontier. The Homestead Act of 1862 did affect the territory, however. The federal government offered 160 acres of frontier land to anyone who would pay a ten-dollar registration fee and farm the land for five years. This began a land rush in the Nebraska Territory. Soon the territory had enough settlers to qualify as a state. In 1867 Nebraska became the thirty-seventh state.

In 1865 the Union Pacific Railroad started building a transcontinental railway west from Omaha across Nebraska. The federal government gave land to the Union Pacific, which the railroad sold to pay for construction. The railroad found buyers by advertising in the United States and Europe for settlers. Many immigrants came from Germany and other northern European countries.

This woodcut shows men working on the Union Pacific Railroad. When the transcontinental line was finished on May 10, 1869, North America became the first continent to have a coast-to-coast railroad line.

15

This special 1866 excursion train transported business tycoons and royalty west on a trip to the 100th meridian. That line of longitude passes through the midpoint of Nebraska, 247 miles west of Omaha.

In eastern and central Nebraska, Native American land titles had been taken over by settlers. But the Sioux and the Cheyenne of western Nebraska decided to fight. Eventually it wasn't the soldiers alone who defeated the Native Americans. It was the buffalo hunters. Professional hunters wiped out the huge herds of buffalo, leaving Native Americans without a very important resource. Finally, the remaining Native American groups were forced to move to the government reservations in North Dakota, South Dakota, Montana, Nebraska, and Oklahoma. The United States government promised they would be cared for.

From 1874 to 1876, plagues of grasshoppers swept through Nebraska, eating all the crops. Many homesteaders decided to head back East. Wagons carried signs such as "Ate out by grasshoppers." By 1878 the

This 1882 photo shows homesteaders in Loup Valley in central Nebraska.

grasshopper plague was over, and the farmers began to return.

In the early 1880s, another land rush brought a new mass of settlers to Nebraska. This drove land prices unrealistically high. Then, in 1890 a drought caused the price of land to collapse. Many farmers were ruined. They blamed the banks and the railroads for mismanaging the state. The Populist party was formed to give farmers a larger voice in government. In 1892 the Populists' candidate for President received eight percent of the vote. As a result the Democratic party adopted many of the Populists' ideas. The Populists supported Nebraskan William Jennings Bryan, the Democratic presidential candidate in 1896. Bryan lost the election, and the Populist party faded away by 1908.

Throughout this period farmers continued to push farther West. New methods of irrigation meant that they could farm land that had once been open range, or grassland. This brought them into conflict with cattle ranchers. The ranchers felt that the land was theirs, whether it was fenced or not. They were accustomed to using the range for their herds. This created range wars in which the farmers and ranchers often settled their differences with violence.

In 1902 Congress passed the Reclamation Act, which provided federal aid for irrigation. This act helped farmers make more profits from the dry lands of the West. Then, in 1904 the Kinkaid Act brought more homesteading to far western Nebraska. Fences went up, and the land was no longer free range. But in the end, the cattlemen won, too. Even with irrigation

Orator William Jennings Bryan ran for President three times but never won. He worked tirelessly to improve the conditions of farmers.

Nebraska's land wasn't suitable for farming. The ranchers eventually bought the homesteaders' land. Western Nebraska was cattle country once again.

In 1917 the United States entered World War I. Nebraska and other farm states profited by the demand for food shipped to troops overseas. Food prices fell after the war ended a year later. The Great Depression of the 1930s dropped the price of farm goods even further. Many farmers who had taken out loans on their land could not pay, and they were forced into bankruptcy. Banks took possession of their land. The problem became worse when an extremely bad drought fell upon the state's western plains. The drought lasted from 1932 to 1937, and the area became part of what was known as the "Dust Bowl." Things got so bad in Nebraska in 1933 that Governor Charles W. Bryan ordered a halt to all farm closings. Later, the federal government stepped in and established long-term, low-interest loans to help the farmers through the bad times.

In 1937 Nebraska tried something new in the way of government. Every other state in the United States had a two-house legislature, a Senate and a House of Representatives. Nebraska decided it needed only a one-house, or unicameral, legislature. Nebraskans felt that laws could be passed quicker by eliminating the debate usually held between sides in a two-house system.

The Dust Bowl drought hit Nebraska so hard that many farming families went bankrupt and were forced to leave the state. Nebraska lost almost five percent of its population.

The United States' entrance into World War II in 1941 brought another boom in farm products. Three years later Congress provided funds for the Missouri River Basin Project. This flood-control project protected the farmlands along the Missouri River valley. In 1948 the Strategic Air Command set up its headquarters at Offutt Air Force Base, outside of Omaha. During the 1950s farms in Nebraska grew bigger and more mechanized. Fewer people were needed to work the land. More and more people began moving to the cities. By 1970 sixty percent of Nebraskans lived in urban areas.

In 1986 Nebraska did something that made the rest of the country take notice. For the first time in the history of the United States, two women ran against each other for the governorship of a state. Kay Orr was the Republican candidate. The Democrat was Helen Boosalis. Orr won the election and became the first Republican woman to be elected a state governor.

Despite attempts to prevent it, the Missouri River and its tributaries flooded in 1993. President Bill Clinton declared parts of Nebraska and eight other states disaster areas. Clinton signed a bill to compensate farmers for their losses. Many farmers were able to begin planting again the next year.

Such strength in the face of disaster is typical of Nebraskans. Throughout their history they have acquired a hardy spirit that often bends but does not break. It is the spirit of Americans who love the land, who planted and reaped and made the land their own.

When Kay Orr was elected in 1986, she became one of only three female governors nationwide.

Homesteaders

People don't settle down in one place for a long time the way they used to. Many people move two or three times in their lifetime. Often these moves are not only across the city or the state, but also across the country. One family made a major move that brought them to Nebraska more than a century ago. But then they stayed, and so did all the generations that followed them.

Wayne and Cathie Belville and their two daughters, Christina and Nancy, work a ranch near Valentine. That is in the Sand Hills area in north-central Nebraska. The ranchland they work today includes the 160 acres Wayne's great-grandparents home-steaded so many years ago.

"My great-grandfather, Benjamin Pearson, had eight brothers and sisters," Wayne said. "As far as I know, he was the only one who came west to homestead. They came out here from Peoria, Illinois. They arrived in

Wayne Belville rides on his family ranch in Nebraska's Sand Hills. His ranch includes the land his great-grandfather homesteaded more than a century ago.

The Belville's ranch provides both their home and their income, but it also ties them closely to their ancestors.

Cherry County in 1884 and home-steaded this location in 1886."

Cherry County is Nebraska's largest county. It is located on the state's northern border. The distance from Peoria to Cherry County is about eight hundred miles. Many pioneers making the trip to the West in the 1880s traveled by covered wagon pulled by horses or oxen. The wagon was usually loaded with as many possessions as would fit. At the rate of 12 to 15 miles a day, it would have taken the Pearsons about two months to make the entire trip.

"When I look at the photographs of my great-great-grandma, sometimes I imagine what it would have been like back then." Nancy said. "I know it must have been really, really hard. Sometimes I wonder how I would have done."

The Pearsons picked out the land they wanted. Their first house was made of sod, or grass-covered soil, just like many Nebraska houses were back then. There was not enough wood on the prairie to build a wooden house. Gradually Wayne's ancestors bought more land around their homestead. Today, the Belvilles own eight thousand acres—fifty times the size of that original plot. The whole ranch is devoted to raising beef cattle.

There's a new generation ready to take over now. Nancy, at 17, hasn't decided what she wants to do. But Christina, 20, is attending college, studying agriculture. She is preparing to deal with the demands of managing the land that's been in her family for more than 150 years.

America's Farmland and More

There are about sixty thousand farms across Nebraska. That figure doesn't tell the whole story, however. Farms cover about 95 percent of the state's land area. That is a larger percentage devoted to farms than any other state has. Nebraska farms range from small, midwestern-style farms in the eastern part of the state to huge cattle ranches in the west. The average-size farm is 856 acres and increasing each year. A farm that size would make a square slightly more than a mile on each side.

The eastern third of Nebraska is cropland. Two thirds of the people in Nebraska live here. The soil is rich, like that in most of the Midwest, and there is enough rainfall to ensure a good crop. Farther west in Nebraska, the weather gets drier. The soil isn't quite as rich as in the eastern part of the state. A larger portion of this area is devoted to ranching.

Beef cattle are Nebraska's single most important agricultural product. They contribute about forty percent of the state's total agricultural income.

Nebraska's largest city, Omaha, is a trade and transportation hub for eastern Nebraska and western Iowa.

A rancher waters cattle on a ranch in the Sand Hills in north-central Nebraska.

Nebraska also raises a large number of hogs, poultry, dairy cattle, and sheep.

Corn is Nebraska's second most important farm product. Much of Nebraska's corn is grown in the fertile eastern part of the state. Some of the irrigated farms in the middle of the state also grow corn. Other major crops in Nebraska are soybeans and wheat. Soybeans are grown in the eastern and central parts of the state. Wheat fields are usually found in the west where dry-farming techniques are applied to nonirrigated fields. Oats, sorghum grain, barley, and rye are also grown in eastern Nebraska. Hay is grown in central Nebraska. Irrigated vegetable farms in the west grow potatoes, onions, and sugar beets. Beekeeping is also a big business in Nebraska. The state's bees produce between five and ten million pounds of honey each year!

Manufacturing accounts for a larger percentage of the state's income than farming does. About 14 percent of Nebraska's income comes from manufacturing, while farming brings in about

With the help of sophisticated irrigation sprinklers, farmers produce 10 percent of Nebraska's gross state product.

10 percent. In Nebraska a large portion of manufacturing's income is related to farm production. By far the single most important area of manufacturing is food processing, especially meat packing. Nebraska has major meat-packing plants in Dakota City, Lexington, Madison, Fremont, and Lincoln. Omaha is the state's largest center for grain processing. Breakfast cereals and livestock feeds are the two principal grain products. Other factories produce baked goods, flour, popcorn, dairy products, and soft drinks.

Omaha and Lincoln account for half of all Nebraska's manufacturing jobs and income. Electrical equipment is manufactured at factories in Omaha, Lincoln, and Columbus. Machinery production, mainly farm machinery, is Nebraska's third largest manufacturing activity.

Can after can of Spam comes off a packaging line at a meat-packing plant. Meat products are Nebraska's most valuable manufactured product.

This man is working on a motorcycle assembly line. Growth in manufacturing is one reason why Nebraska has one of the lowest unemployment rates in the nation.

Omaha and Lincoln are also the foundation of the state's service industries. Nearly two thirds of Nebraska's annual income is derived from services of some kind. Service industries are those in which workers serve other people instead of making a product. Service workers work in many places, including department stores, banks, and insurance companies.

The main service industries in Nebraska are finance, insurance, and real estate. The Mutual of Omaha Insurance Company is the world's largest private health insurance company. Omaha is also home to Berkshire Hathaway, a financial giant that owns many other companies. Wholesale and retail trade is the second largest Nebraska service industry. These are businesses that sell things, either to other businesses or to individual customers. Another major service industry in Nebraska is social and personal services. This is the sort of professional help you'd get from a law firm, a hospital, or an auto repair shop. Government is an important service industry, too. The headquarters of the United States Strategic Command is at Offutt Air Force Base, near Omaha.

Tourism is another major economic activity in Nebraska and it is growing fast. More than 15 million people spend more than two billion dollars in the state every year. Nebraska's pioneer heritage is on display in many popular museums and historical sites. The state also has 78 state outdoor recreation areas, including 8 state parks and 8 state historical parks. In addition Nebraska hosts several of the nation's largest rodeos and dozens of smaller ones. Rodeos showcase traditional cowboy skills, such as calf roping and bronco riding. Omaha and Lincoln have their share of art museums, shopping areas, and other tourist attractions.

In the 1990s Nebraska's land values rose slightly, and crop and livestock prices remained high. These are signs of healthy and prosperous farms. The outlook is also good for manufacturing industries that rely on agricultural products. This news is all the more satisfying considering Nebraska's harsh and unruly climate. Nebraska has droughts in some years, and in other years it has floods. In addition hailstorms, tornadoes, blizzards, and violent thunderstorms happen in the state annually. It is clear that Nebraska farmers must be industrious and creative to succeed in spite of such conditions. With so many jobs dependent on agriculture, their success is Nebraska's success, too.

Creative packaging of its pioneer heritage is helping Nebraska become a major tourist attraction. Here, frontier life is re-created at Homestead National Monument, near Beatrice in southeastern Nebraska.

A New Life in a Small Town

In 1985 Dannebrog, Nebraska, was a town in trouble. Dannebrog is a small community of 324 people located in central Nebraska. That was the year market prices for crops and livestock were at an all-time low. Farmers who lived near the town were struggling to feed their families. Dannebrog was feeling the same financial pinch as the farmers were because fewer local farmers were coming to town to buy groceries and supplies. Eventually the Dannebrog bank closed, and many other businesses were on the point of closing. But sometimes people are at their best when things look their worst. The citizens of Dannebrog rallied together and figured out a strategy to save the town.

First, several local businessmen pooled their money and opened a credit union, a small financial institution that loans money to people. Shirley Johnson and her husband borrowed money to move their grocery store to a larger building. Harriett Nielson borrowed money to open a Danish restaurant. A Danish signpainting business and several gift shops selling Danish crafts also opened. After nine months the credit union was doing so well that a nearby bank bought it. Dannebrog citizens were grateful for the financial security that the bank provided.

Meanwhile some of the citizens had formed a Booster Club to call attention to the town. The town's

In 1989 Dannebrog persuaded the Nebraska legislature to name it the "Danish Capital of Nebraska."

Two Dannebrog artists painted this mural in 1991. The mural is a monument to Dannebrog's historical and ethnic background.

one-hundred-year birthday was in 1986, and Dannebrog decided to publicize it. The residents then organized a yearly spring festival held on the first weekend of June. The festival features a parade, an arts and crafts sale, traditional Danish dancers, and, of course, Danish food. Tourists soon began discovering the town.

Then the people of Dannebrog had an incredible stroke of luck. Roger Welsch and his family lived on a farm a few miles outside of town. Welsch was a friend of Charles Kuralt, then the host of CBS-TV's *Sunday Morning*. In 1988 Kuralt asked Welsch to do a short segment twice a month for his television show. It would be called "Postcard from Nebraska," and it would feature Welsch talking about Dannebrog and the surrounding area. Since then "Postcard" has become one of the show's most popular features. "Now our problem is giving the tourists something to do once they get here," Shirley Johnson laughs.

Dannebrog is a living example of what can be done with teamwork and love for a hometown. Maybe none of the residents knew what a wonderful town they lived in until there was trouble. Maybe all of them knew—and now all of America knows it, too.

Art from the Endless Prairie

Nebraska is a wide expanse of prairie. At first glance the land seems to lack drama. It doesn't boast a rocky seacoast, towering mountains, or majestic forests. Yet Nebraska is a place that creates drama, and from drama comes culture. Nebraska's summers are blisteringly hot, and its winters are harsh and cold. Rainfall is scarce. In the early days, these conditions meant toil and sacrifice for the inhabitants. Their struggles yielded rich crops and herds. They also inspired many talented writers to capture Nebraska's landscape, climate, and heritage in their art.

Willa Cather, one of the United States' finest novelists, was born in Virginia in 1873. She moved to Red Cloud, Nebraska, when she was nine years old. Cather came to love the immigrant pioneers whose strength and hard work were taming the prairie.

From that love Cather wrote her classic American novels *O Pioneers!* and *My Ántonia*. In 1923 she was awarded the Pulitzer Prize in fiction for *One of Ours*, another story set in Nebraska. Her books celebrate

Willa Cather wrote 12 novels and is considered by many to be one of America's best writers. She also worked as the editor of a magazine, a position rarely held by women in her day.

Susette La Flesche wrote about and painted her Native American people. She also toured the country, generating support for respect of tribal lands.

people who love their land and tell how the land strengthened them. Her female characters have an independent spirit that sets them apart from earlier portrayals of women in fiction.

Susette La Flesche, who lived from 1854 to 1903, was a writer and a painter. She was also the daughter of an Omaha chief. Her paintings show scenes from Native American life in Nebraska through the eyes of a Native American woman. La Flesche worked to better her people under the name of "Bright Eyes," the English translation of her Native American name, *Inshta Theumba*. She gave speeches throughout the United States and Great Britain against removing Native Americans from their traditional lands.

Still another notable writer was Mari Sandoz. She was born in northwestern Nebraska and lived from 1901 to 1966. She grew up playing with Native American children. One of her best-known works is a history of the state called *Love Song to the Plains*. In it she describes the daily lives of Nebraska's ranchers, homesteaders, and Native Americans. She also wrote two children's books about Sioux life, *The Horse Catcher* and *The Story Catcher*.

Of course Nebraska has produced well-known male authors as well. Susette La Flesche's brother Francis La Flesche also wrote and worked for Native American rights. He was a scholar who created a dictionary of the Osage language and a history of the Omaha nation. He also wrote several other books about Native Americans, including the story of his life. C. W. Anderson wrote and illustrated books about horses. He was born in Wahoo, forty miles west of Omaha. He is best known for his *Billy and Blaze* children's series. He used his own horses as the models for some of the horses in his books.

Another Nebraskan author was John G. Neihardt. He moved to the state in 1891 at the age of ten. As a young man, he lived with the Omaha people, and Native American life was a strong feature in his work. Neihardt is best known for *Black Elk Speaks*. This book is based on a series of interviews with Black Elk, an elderly Sioux holy man. The book records oral traditions of Sioux religion and philosophy. If this book had not been written, much of that wisdom might have been lost forever.

Nebraska has made a great contribution in the area of performing arts. A surprising number of gifted show people have come from a relatively small population.

Even though the famous scout and showman "Buffalo Bill" Cody was born in Iowa, he lived much of his life near North Platte, Nebraska. In the 1860s he was a pony express rider. Later, he hunted buffalo to feed the crews building the first railroad across the United States. In 1882 he turned to show business and staged the "Old Glory Blowout" in North Platte. It was the first commercial rodeo ever held. The next year he organized Buffalo Bill's Wild West Show, a touring troupe of trick riders, sharpshooters, and ropers. For over thirty years, he and his show toured the United States and Europe. One of his stars was sharpshooter Annie Oakley.

This is a dramatic painting Susette La Flesche did to illustrate a book on Nebraska history.

This is "Buffalo Bill" Cody's home at Scouts Rest Ranch, near North Platte. Many members of his troupe spent the winter months on this four-thousand-acre ranch.

Any list of Hollywood stars from Nebraska has to start with Marlon Brando and Henry Fonda. Brando's realistic style has made him one of the great actors of the last fifty years. He won Best Actor Oscars for his roles in *On the Waterfront* (1954) and *The Godfather* (1972). In a career spanning more than fifty years, Fonda appeared in more than eighty films. He won an Oscar for his last film, *On Golden Pond* (1981).

Fred Astaire, who gracefully danced his way through more than 35 movie musicals, belongs on the list of Nebraska's stars. So does Nick Nolte, star of *48 HRS.* and many other recent films, who was born in Omaha. Among television personalities, talk show hosts Johnny Carson and Dick Cavett both come from Nebraska.

Nebraska's culture is reflected in several outstanding museums. In Omaha, for example, the Joslyn Art Museum houses one of the nation's best collections of Western American art. The University of Nebraska in Lincoln has two large art museums. The Museum of Nebraska History, also in Lincoln, is the state's major history museum. The Great Plains Black History Museum in Omaha has the largest collection of items relating to African American history west of the Mississippi.

From major literary figures to great performers, Nebraska's spreading plains have nurtured a wide range of remarkable talent. Its soil has proved as fertile for our nation's culture as it has for the corn and cattle that feed us.

Annie Oakley, one of the best rifle shots in the country, was a star of Buffalo Bill's Wild West Show.

Johnny Carson hosted *The Tonight Show* for thirty years, from 1962 to 1992.

Another Chance

In the late twentieth century, adolescent crime, violence, and drug abuse have skyrocketed into a national crisis. But there's a place near Omaha that is remarkably effective at helping thousands of at-risk young people. What's more this place has been doing its work for nearly eighty years. The name of this place is Boys Town.

The story of Boys Town begins in Omaha with Father Edward Flanagan, a 31-year-old Roman Catholic priest. Father Flanagan planned to start a shelter for homeless and neglected boys. He borrowed ninety dollars and rented a two-story, brick building for that purpose. Father Flanagan had previously provided a shelter for homeless men. Many of them were criminals, alcoholics, and drug addicts. Gradually Father Flanagan decided the men were too old to change their ways. "If you want to repair a building," he said, "you must begin before the decay sets in too deeply." His home for boys was based on the idea that "To save children from crime is to end crime."

Father Edward Flanagan founded Boys Town after his work with homeless boys outgrew two homes in Omaha.

The brick home that became Father Flanagan's Home for Boys on December 12, 1917, had room for 25 boys. The first residents under Father Flanagan's care were three homeless orphans and two young criminals assigned to him by the juvenile court.

Father Flanagan asked nearly everyone in town for donations to help pay the bills. Some parishioners and a few Omaha businessmen believed in what he was doing and donated some money. Those who could not give money often provided food or old clothing.

Father Flanagan's Home for Boys was based on two ideals. The first was that Boys Town would turn no one away. The second ideal was that there is no such thing as a "bad boy." "These aren't bad boys," he'd say over and over again. "They've just never been loved." Instead of punishing a boy who fought or became destructive, Father Flanagan told him how good the boy was inside. "Most boys want to do what's right," he said. "They want to be praised and admired. But sometimes they don't know the right way to win praise, and they do the wrong things. You have to show them, by training and example, what is the right way."

This simple method developed by a gentle and loving man was outstandingly successful. Within six months Father Flanagan's shelter was home to fifty boys. They were sleeping on portable cots in every room and the basement. Father Flanagan found a building that would sleep a hundred and rented it. Soon that building was full, too!

Then Father Flanagan heard of a ninety-acre farm for sale out on the prairie, 15 miles west of Omaha. The

This famous statue, with its inscription, "He ain't heavy, Father . . . he's m' brother," symbolizes the caring and familylike love generations of boys have found at Boys Town.

In 1917 Father Flanagan opened his first home for boys in this house in Omaha, known as the "House on Dodge Street."

price of the farm was far out of his range. Eventually Father Flanagan appealed to the owner's kindness, and the two men agreed on a price. Father Flanagan and his boys moved onto the farm on October 22, 1921. The name given to the sprawling former farm was "Boys Town."

Father Flanagan died in 1948, but by that time he'd built a solid organization dedicated to caring for boys in trouble. Today, Boys Town is a multi-million-dollar organization, and the original "town" has grown to more than one thousand acres.

For many years the boys were housed in buildings that provided each with his own room or apartment. In 1974 this arrangement was replaced by one involving family-style homes. Each of these homes provide shelter and stability for six to eight children supervised by a specially trained adult married couple. Being guides, counselors, supervisors, and "parents" for the children is truly a full-time job. The children are expected to attend school, do homework, and share in family chores. It is hoped that through this process the children will develop responsibility and self-control.

Boys Town began accepting girls in 1979. Today, the name "Boys Town" stands for the town itself and the entire organization. Boys Town is the home of 556 young residents living in

76 homes. The town also includes school buildings, workshops, a gym, and other buildings.

Boys Town also operates homes at 17 locations in 11 states and the District of Columbia. These out-of-state sites are usually a cluster of five family-style homes in a neighborhood setting. A few of the sites are individual homes. The children's care in these out-of-state sites is organized in the same way as at Boys Town.

Throughout its long history, Boys Town has provided a shining example of the success that can be achieved by the power of love. Today, it is also a model for the future.

Boys Town operates a national hotline and provides homes for neglected and homeless children of all races and religions.

Father Peter, the executive director of Boys Town, appears with some of the children Boys Town has helped.

The Trail of Progress

Can you imagine life in the days of covered wagons, steam locomotives, and mail delivery by pony express? Some people say those were "the good old days," when life was simple. Others see those days as a time of hardship. In either case Harold Warp believed it was important to preserve things from those horse-and-buggy days. He is the founder of Pioneer Village in Minden.

More than fifty thousand items are on display in the buildings that house the exhibits. They surround a village green, all within less than a mile walk. Visitors usually begin in the main building, which holds more than ten thousand items arranged in chronological order. From early plows and wagons to modern threshers and snowmobiles, progress is on display.

After the main building, visitors can stop at Elm Creek Fort, the first log cabin in Webster County, and go on to a replica of a general store filled with merchandise. They can proceed to a train depot, a fully furnished house made of sod, and more homes and shops from the past. Often there are demonstrations of broom making, glass blowing, rug weaving, blacksmithing, and other early crafts.

Advancement in transportation is represented by hundreds of antique cars, carriages, and bicycles. Visitors can climb aboard a railroad locomotive or an old street car. The collection of flying machines includes an early jet and a helicopter. Farm machinery is well-represented, too—from hand-powered machines to

Pictured here are the china shop and the church at Pioneer Village. The china shop contains some glass and china pieces that were originally transported to Nebraska in covered wagons.

Pioneer Village is one of Nebraska's most popular tourist attractions.

ox-powered, horse-powered, and self-propelled machines. Firefighting equipment ranges from handcarts to the modern fire truck.

Antique pianos and other musical instruments are on display, along with the earliest phonographs and radios. In the toy shop, visitors can view cast-iron toys, handmade dolls, baby carriages, and other popular toys from the past. Hobbyists can spend days browsing through the collections. There are household items, jewelry, model cars, and toy trains.

The country school may well be the founder's favorite place. It is furnished with desks, books, stove,

dinner pails, and more. It even has Harold Warp's "Perfect Attendance" certificates on display!

Born and raised in Nebraska, Harold Warp once compared our world to "a sleeping giant" who was awakened. "In a mere hundred and fifty years . . . , man progressed from open hearths, grease lamps, and oxcarts to television, supersonic speed and atomic power. . . ." Warp planned Pioneer Village as a tribute to our nation's past as well as a celebration of its astounding progress. Through these amazing collections, he has preserved the achievements of our nation for generations to come.

Farming in the Future

Every year it becomes more expensive to farm. Farming has become an energy-intensive industry. Tractors, combines, and other farm equipment all run on diesel fuel. Not only do fuel prices keep going up, but so do machinery prices. From the mid-1970s through the 1980s, the market prices for crops and livestock stayed low. Even though the farmers' costs went up every year, the price of their crops stayed low. Farmers had a hard time making enough money. When farms are hurting financially, the economy of the entire state is also hurt.

Fortunately, since the late 1980s, things have improved. Fuel prices have stayed steady and sometimes even dropped. The market prices for farm crops and ranch livestock have been rising slowly but steadily. From 1989 through the mid-1990s, the average income per farm increased by more than ten percent. In addition the amount the average farmer owes, compared to the value of the land, has dropped in recent years.

The Joslyn Art Museum in Omaha features both traditional art and futuristic modern art.

More than nearly any other state, Nebraska's economic future is tied to the success or failure of farms such as this one.

Nebraska is now facing a problem that could get worse in the future. Much of the state is too dry to farm without irrigation. Some of the water comes from rivers, especially the North Platte River. But dams in neighboring states have reduced the flow from the North Platte River by two thirds even before the water reaches Nebraska! If water does not come from rivers, it must come from aquifers, which are natural pools of water deep underground. Until recently not much thought has been given to how long these aquifers could supply water. Aquifers are a nonrenewable resource, which means the water cannot be replaced. Irrigation and municipal water supplies have reduced the size of Nebraska's aquifers.

Today, water conservation is a major concern in the state. Everyone is being encouraged to take shorter showers, sprinkle their lawns less, and wash their cars less often. In addition farmers are learning ways to grow more crops with less water.

It is too soon to tell how well these measures are working. It is likely that other changes will be needed, too. For Nebraska to remain a major farm state, it may either have to find another source for water or change the way the land is farmed. Perhaps a combination of both solutions is possible. In any case the issue is now before the people of Nebraska. The answer is waiting in the twenty-first century.

1541 Francisco Vásquez de Coronado lays claim to the entire Southwest, including present-day Nebraska.

1682 René-Robert Cavelier, Sieur de La Salle, travels down the Mississippi River. He claims all the land drained by the river for France, including the Nebraska area.

1714 Etienne Veniard de Bourgmont travels up the Missouri River to the Platte River.

1720 Pedro de Villasur's forces are defeated by the Pawnee.

1739 Pierre and Paul Mallet explore the Missouri and Platte rivers.

1803 The United States acquires the Nebraska area as part of the Louisiana Purchase.

1804 Meriwether Lewis and William Clark explore the Missouri River.

1806 Zebulon Pike visits what is now south-central Nebraska.

1809 Manuel Lisa begins building trading posts along the Missouri River.

1813 Robert Stuart crosses Nebraska on his way from Oregon to New York. This route later becomes the Oregon Trail.

1819 Fort Atkinson is built.

1823 Bellevue is founded as a trading post.

1843 Settlers begin traveling across Nebraska along the Oregon Trail.

1854 Nebraska is incorporated as a United States territory.

1862 Congress passes the Homestead Act, which increases settlement in the territory.

1865 The Union Pacific Railroad begins building west from Omaha.

1867 Nebraska becomes the thirty-seventh state.

1872 The nation's first Arbor Day is celebrated in Nebraska as a way of increasing the number of trees on the prairie.

1877 The Sioux surrender at Fort Robinson.

1902 Congress passes the Reclamation Act, which provides irrigation for western homesteaders.

1904 Congress passes the Kinkaid Act.

1930s Severe droughts and high winds blow away much of the state's topsoil.

1933 The governor declares a halt on farm foreclosures.

1937 Nebraska changes to a unicameral legislature.

1939 Oil is discovered in eastern Nebraska.

1944 Congress approves the Missouri River Basin Project.

1952 The Missouri River overflows in one of the state's worst floods.

1967 The Nebraska Department of Economic Development is established to attract new industry.

1985 The value of farmland plummets. Many farmers lose their farms. Record infestations of grasshoppers hit the Great Plains, and millions of acres of cropland are destroyed.

1986 Republican Kay Orr and Democrat Helen Boosalis run against each other for governor.

1993 After the Missouri River floods, President Bill Clinton declares parts of Nebraska and eight other states disaster areas.

The state flag is deep blue, with the state seal in gold in the center. On the seal a blacksmith with a hammer and anvil represents industry. Agriculture is symbolized by a settler's cabin, sheaves of harvested wheat, and stalks of growing corn. A steamboat and a railroad train stand for the forms of transportation that brought settlers to Nebraska. The Rocky Mountains rise in the background.

Nebraska Almanac

Nickname. The Cornhusker State

Capital. Lincoln

State Bird. Western meadowlark

State Flower. Goldenrod

State Tree. Cottonwood

State Motto. Equality Before the Law

State Song. "Beautiful Nebraska"

State Abbreviations. Neb. (traditional); NE (postal)

Statehood. March 1, 1867, the 37th state

Government. Congress: U.S. senators, 2; U.S. representatives, 3. State Legislature: senators, 49; representatives, none (the legislature has only one house). Counties: 93

Area. 77,359 sq mi (200,358 sq km), 15th in size among the states

Greatest Distances. north/south, 206 mi (331 km); east/west, 462 mi (743 km)

Elevation. Highest: 5,426 ft (1,654 m), in Kimball County. Lowest: 840 ft (256 m), in Richardson County

Population. 1990 Census: 1,584,617 (1% increase over 1980), 36th among the states. Density: 20 persons per sq mi (8 persons per sq km). Distribution: 66% urban, 34% rural. 1980 Census: 1,569,825

Economy. *Agriculture:* beef cattle, corn, hogs and pigs, soybeans, wheat, poultry, dairy cattle, oats, sorghum, hay, sheep, honey, beans, potatoes, sugar beets, onions. *Manufacturing:* food products, electric and electronic equipment, machinery, printed materials, chemicals, fabricated metal products. *Mining:* petroleum, sand and gravel, clay, limestone

State Seal

State Bird: Western meadowlark

State Flower: Goldenrod

Annual Events

★ Arbor Day celebrations (April)

★ Days of '56 Rodeo and Celebration in Ponca (June)

★ Nebraskaland Days in North Platte (June)

★ Arrows to Aerospace Celebration in Bellevue (June/July)

★ Nightly Rodeo in North Platte (June/July)

★ Oregon Trail Days in Gering (July)

★ Winnebago Pow Wow in Winnebago (July)

★ Nebraska's Biggest Rodeo in Burwell (August)

★ Nebraska State Fair in Lincoln (August/September)

Places to Visit

★ Arbor Lodge in Nebraska City

★ Buffalo Bill Ranch State Historical Park, near North Platte

★ Chimney Rock National Historical Site, near Bayard

★ DeSoto National Wildlife Refuge, near Blair

★ Fort Kearney State Historical Park, near Kearney

★ Great Plains Black History Museum in Omaha

★ Homestead National Monument, near Beatrice

★ Museum of Nebraska History in Lincoln

★ Pioneer Village, near Minden

★ Scotts Bluff National Monument, near Fort Robinson

★ Stuhr Museum of the Prairie Pioneer, near Grand Island

★ Willa Cather Historical Center in Red Cloud

Index